The Jamestown Colony

by Deanne Kells

Table of Contents

Introduction 2
Chapter 1 How Did Jamestown Begin? 4
Chapter 2 What Was Jamestown Like? 8
Chapter 3 What Happened
to Jamestown? 14
Summary 20
Glossary 22
Index 24

❧ Introduction ☙

Jamestown was a **colony** in **North America**. Jamestown was also a **community**. People live and work together in a community.

▲ This is what Jamestown looked like.

Read about the Jamestown community.

Words to Know

- colonists
- colony
- community
- government
- Jamestown
- North America
- tobacco

See the Glossary on page 22.

Chapter 1

How Did Jamestown Begin?

Three ships sailed from England. The ships sailed in 1607. The ships sailed to North America. Men and boys were on the ships.

▲ Three ships sailed to North America.

The Virginia Company sent the ships. The company wanted a colony in North America. The company wanted gold.

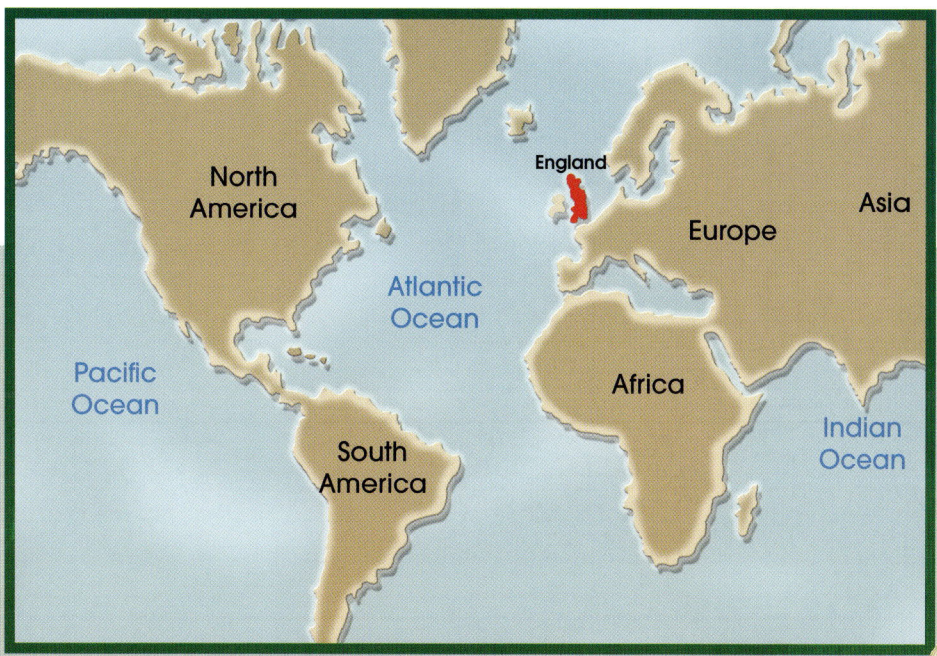

▲ These are the seals of the Virginia Company.

Chapter 1

The men and boys built Jamestown. Jamestown was a colony. The men and boys were **colonists**.

▲ The colonists built Jamestown.

How Did Jamestown Begin?

The colonists looked for gold.

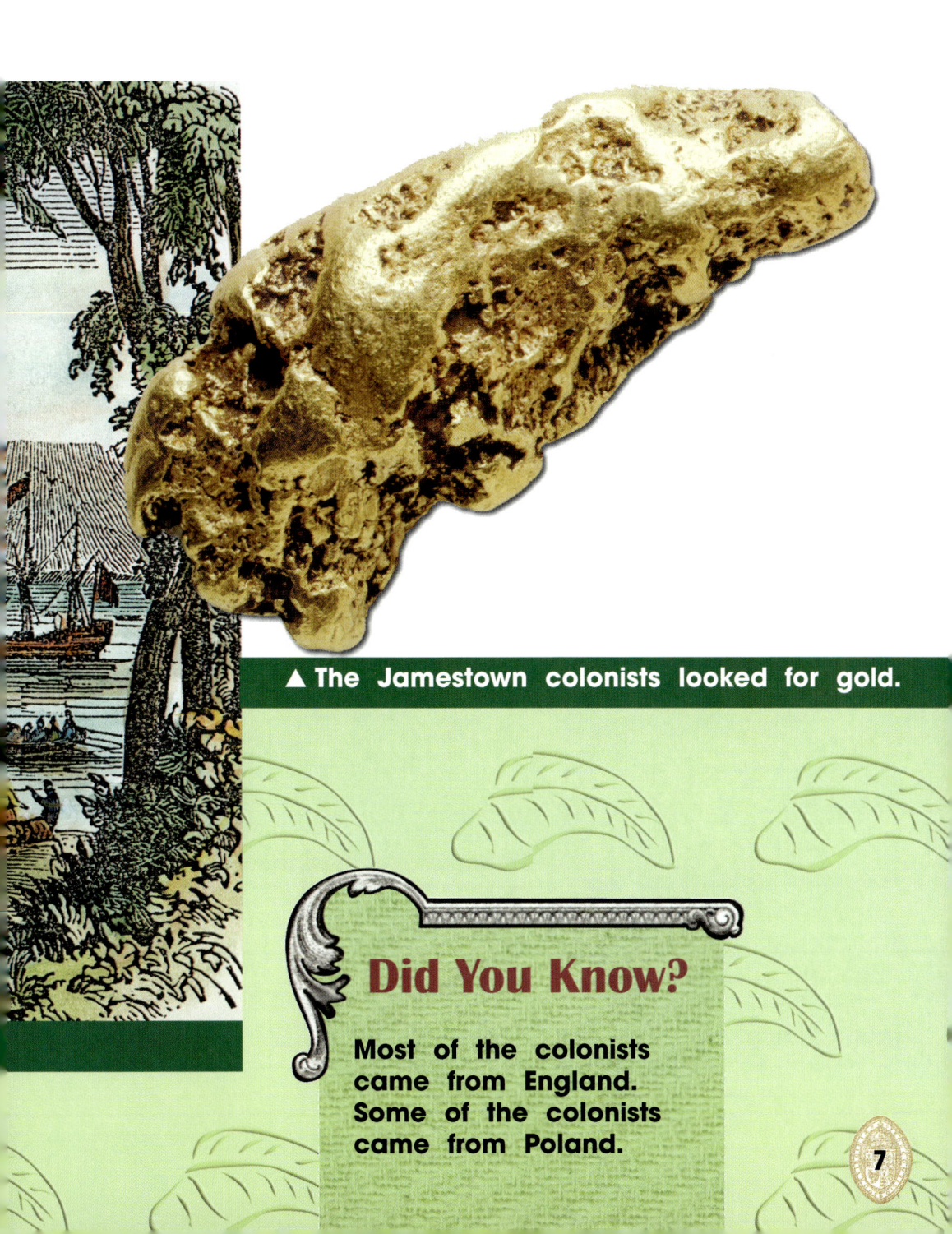

▲ The Jamestown colonists looked for gold.

Did You Know?

Most of the colonists came from England. Some of the colonists came from Poland.

Chapter 2

What Was Jamestown Like?

The colonists thought the land was beautiful. The land was also very wet. Mosquitoes lived in the wet land. Mosquitoes made the colonists sick.

▲ The colonists thought the land around Jamestown was beautiful.

Solve This

104 men and boys settled in Jamestown. About half of them died the first year. About how many of them lived?

Answer: about 52

▲ Mosquitoes made colonists sick.

The water at Jamestown was salty. The water was not good to drink. The water made colonists sick.

▲ Colonists got sick from the water.

▲ The Powhatan lived near Jamestown.

It's a Fact Native Americans lived near Jamestown. The Native Americans were the Powhatan. Sometimes the Powhatan were friendly. Sometimes the Powhatan attacked the colonists.

Chapter 2

Some colonists did not want to plant crops. Some colonists did not want to build houses. Those colonists just wanted to dig for gold.

▲ Colonists wanted to dig for gold.

What Was Jamestown Like?

John Smith was a leader of Jamestown. John Smith said colonists must plant crops. John Smith said colonists must build houses.

▲ John Smith

People to Know

John Smith was a good leader. Smith made the colonists work.

People to Know

Pocahontas was the daughter of the Powhatan chief. Pocahontas helped the colonists. She helped John Smith.

▲ Pocahontas

Chapter 2

John Smith was hurt in 1609. He went back to England.

▲ John Smith returned to England.

What Was Jamestown Like?

The winter of 1609-1610 was very bad. Many colonists did not have enough food. Many colonists were sick. Many colonists died.

▲ The winter of 1609-1610 was the Starving Time.

Chapter 3

What Happened to Jamestown?

The colonists wanted to make money. Finally the colonists planted **tobacco**. People in England wanted tobacco. The colonists sold the tobacco to England.

▲ The colonists planted tobacco.

People to Know

John Rolfe was the first colonist to plant tobacco. John Rolfe married Pocahontas.

▲ John Rolfe and Pocahontas got married.

The colonists started a **government** in 1619. The government made laws for the colony.

▲ Only men were in the government.

Chapter 3

Women came to Jamestown in 1619. The women came to be wives. Now the colonists had families.

▲ The Virginia Company sent women to Jamestown.

What Happened to Jamestown?

Africans came to Jamestown in 1619. The Africans were servants. They worked and became free. Then the Africans owned their land.

▲ Africans came to Jamestown.

It's a Fact
Most of the Africans were slaves by 1661.

Chapter 3

The king of England wanted Jamestown. The king made Jamestown his colony in 1624.

▲ James I was king of England.

What Happened to Jamestown?

The government moved away from Jamestown in 1699. Then, many colonists left Jamestown. Jamestown was no longer there.

Then & Now

About 70,000 people lived in Jamestown in 1699. Now Jamestown is a historic place. People do not live there.

▲ People rebuilt the Jamestown houses.

Summary

Colonists came to North America for gold. The colonists built Jamestown. Jamestown became a community. Jamestown was no longer there by 1750.

May 14, 1607
The first colonists came to Jamestown.

1612
John Rolfe grew tobacco.

Winter of 1609-1610
Many colonists died.

1619
- Jamestown started its own government.
- The Virginia Company sent women to Jamestown.
- The first Africans came to Jamestown.

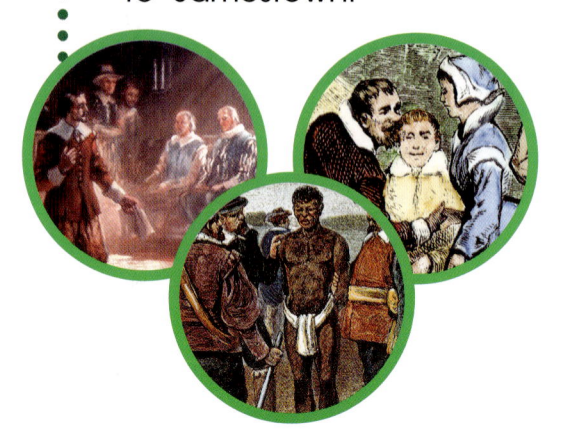

1624
The king of England wanted Jamestown.

1750
Jamestown was no longer there.

1699
The government moved away from Jamestown.

Think About It

1. Why did John Smith say colonists must work?

2. What was the Starving Time?

Glossary

colonists people who live in colonies

Colonists built Jamestown.

colony a place owned by another country

Jamestown was a colony.

community a place where people live and work

Jamestown was also a community.

government the laws of a community

Jamestown started a government.

Jamestown a colony in North America

*The king of England wanted **Jamestown**.*

North America a continent

*Jamestown was in **North America**.*

tobacco a plant with leaves that people smoke

*The colonists planted **tobacco** crops.*

Index

Africans, 17, 20
colonists, 6–11, 13–16, 19–21
colony, 2, 5–6, 15, 18
community, 2–3, 20
England, 4, 7, 12, 14, 18, 21
gold, 5, 7, 10, 20
government, 15, 19, 21
Jamestown, 2–3, 6–9, 11, 16–21
King James I, 18, 21
mosquitoes, 8
North America, 2, 4–5, 20
Pocahontas, 11, 14
Powhatan, 9, 11
Rolfe, John, 14, 20
ships, 4–5
slaves, 17
Smith, John, 11–12, 21
Starving Time, 13, 21
tobacco, 14, 20
Virginia Company, 5, 16, 20
water, 9
women, 16, 20